The Football Association has developed a soccer education programme for you - the young player whether you are a boy or girl - The Coca-Cola Football Association Soccer Star Scheme.

The scheme is about developing your ability in the critical soccer techniques of:

- ★ Running with the ball
- ★ Changing direction with and without the ball
- ★ Dribbling
- ★ Heading
- ★ Shooting
- ★ Passing and Control.

To focus your attention towards these techniques and for you to be able to measure your progress we have developed a series of enjoyable challenges: The Soccer Star Tests.

To master the techniques and score highly on the Soccer Star Tests follow this programme.

1 Watch good players - at live matches, on television and particularly by studying the Soccer Star Video.

2 To assess your ability test yourself, or be tested by your coach, teacher, parent, or youth leader. Check your results with the tables shown at the end of this book. The tests and tables are the same for both boys and girls.

3 You will now discover which techniques you can perform better than others and which areas need to be improved. Set **yourself** a target; an objective to aim for to achieve when you are next tested.

4 Have fun by following the recommended practices and games in this book and on the Soccer Star Video. These practices will guide you towards:

- ★ improving your performance in those techniques you need to develop.

- ★ maintaining your progress in those areas in which you are already proficient.

5 Whilst parents, teachers and coaches can help you; **you** must take the responsibility for your progress. Be all you can be - by practising as much and as often as possible. If you are in doubt check out this book, the video or ask your parents, teacher, youth leader or coach for advice.

6 When you feel you are ready to be tested - once, twice, three or even four times a year - then this should be organised by your teacher, coach or youth leader.

Once you have been tested record your results on the appropriate page, in this book and on receipt of your scores you will be sent the following:-

★ Your Soccer Star Certificate
★ Your Soccer Star Cloth Badge
★ Your Soccer Star Bag Sticker
★ Your individual Soccer Star Progress Report
★ Your Soccer Stars to use on page 64.

Your individual progress report will outline your own strengths and weaknesses and direct you towards your future soccer development. There are six grades in the Soccer Star Scheme and so there is an opportunity for all young players to progress. If you reach the 6 star grade - the Champion Class - this will indicate you are in the top one per cent of all players for your age in your country, and on reaching this level we will recommend you for a trial at your local Football League Club's Centre of Excellence.

Developing good techniques is part of the process in becoming a better soccer player but so is developing the right attitudes. It is important therefore that at all times you follow the Code of Conduct as shown on page 4.

Commit yourself to our Scheme and this Code of Conduct by completing the personal details below.

NAME OF PLAYER: _____

ADDRESS OF PLAYER: _____

_____

_____

DATE OF BIRTH: _____

SCHOOL: _____

CLUB: _____

Coca-Cola in Great Britain is delighted to support The Soccer Star Scheme as part of the Coca-Cola Football Association Coaching and Educational Scheme.

Coca-Cola has supported youth football in Great Britain for over ten years as sponsors of the former Coca-Cola Football Association Superskills Awards.

Internationally, The Coca-Cola Company recognises the popularity of youth football and operates sponsorship programmes in many of the 155 countries in which "Coca-Cola" is sold. The Company is the worldwide sponsor of the FIFA/Coca-Cola Cup, World Youth Championships.

In Great Britain, Coca-Cola supports many other sports in addition to football. By working in association with official bodies Coca-Cola promotes the teaching of basic skills in a variety of sports. There are Coca-Cola Youth programmes in gymnastics, tennis, swimming and golf, currently operating in schools and leisure centres throughout the country.

'Coca-Cola' is a registered trade mark of The Coca-Cola Company.

THE SOCCER STAR SCHEME CODE OF CONDUCT

DO

★ Study the Laws of the Game and adhere to them at **all** times.
★ Practise and improve your soccer techniques in order to beat your opponents by skilful not unfair methods.
★ Play to win and enjoy yourself but be sure to take victory modestly and defeat graciously.
★ When playing or watching, praise skilful play by both teams.
★ Strive to set standards of behaviour for others to follow: standards of punctuality, politeness and appearance eg, keep your soccer boots and kit clean!

DON'T

★ Argue with the Referee or Linesmen.
★ Attempt to 'referee' the game by appealing for throw-ins, free kicks, offsides, etc.
★ Lose your self control and retaliate.
★ Forget to retire 10 yards quickly when a free kick is given against you.
★ Over-react when your team scores a goal.

Please be sure to encourage your friends to have a greater respect for soccer and for all those involved in it. By following the Code of Conduct you will be a credit to your parents, your school, your club and, most of all, yourself.

As a result of your successful instruction you now have the opportunity to wear the badge of The Soccer Star Scheme. Wear it with pride and do nothing in your conduct on or off the field to dishonour this badge.

The Soccer Star Scheme Code of Conduct	**4**
A message to all Parents, Teachers, Coaches and Youth Leaders	**6**
Running with the ball	**8**
Turning	**12**
Speed	**23**
Dribbling	**26**
Heading	**32**
Shooting	**37**
Passing and Control	**44**
Small-sided Games	**46**
Score Tables	**48-61**
The Pennant Offer	**63**
Recording Star Grades	**65**

The Soccer Star Scheme and this book were devised and written by: ROBIN M. RUSSELL.
Editorial Assistant: SUE BARWICK.
Graphic Design and Artwork: JOHN E. HALLDEARN.
Front Cover Computer Graphics: IMAGINE.
Front Cover Design: PATRICK KNOWLES.
Photography: BOB THOMAS SPORTS PHOTOGRAPHY.
Typesetting: JETSET TYPESETTING LTD.
Printing: TINSLEY ROBOR LABELS LTD.,
    Commercial Print Division.

© The Football Association 1988

All rights reserved. No part of this publication may be reproduced, stored in a retrieval system, or transmitted in any form or by any means, electronic, mechanical, photocopying, recording or otherwise, without the permission of the copyright holder.

A MESSAGE TO ALL COACHES/TEACHERS/ PARENTS and YOUTH LEADERS.

WHAT TO LEARN?

The techniques identified in this book for young players to learn have been identified through Match Performance Analysis. These techniques are direct, dynamic and are not static exercises, like ball juggling.

HOW TO LEARN THE TECHNIQUES?

Adults and youngsters are recommended to use The Soccer Star Video produced in association with this book and follow the following programme:

i) **The Start: Interest, Inspiration and Imitation**

   By watching the match action on the video and through seeing good players play live or on television, the imagination of the child will be captured. Outstanding performances from older players and the youngsters on the Soccer Star Video will also inspire the young player towards imitating good examples.

ii) **How to maintain this interest: The Assessment Test**

   ★ Get the children to have a go at the tests and challenges as part of the Soccer Star Scheme. They should enjoy the sheer fun of the activity. The tests themselves have been devised in conjunction with the University of Southampton Department of Social Statistics. Following a lengthy period of examination, the test-retest reliability for the combination of all tests, was found to be in excess of 90%. Furthermore by comparing the test scores with widely different ability groups, the overall validity of the tests was determined to be approximately 85%.

   ★ Record the players' scores on the column on the Record Sheet marked 'Assessment Test'.

   ★ These tests will then focus the attention of the child and the adult volunteers towards the specific areas necessary for improvement. New objectives can be set and progress measured.

   ★ In maintaining interest, achieving **early** success is vital in reinforcing good habits.

iii) **How to achieve early success**

   ★ In association with the video accentuate the positive - the DOs and avoid the bad habits of the DON'Ts.

   ★ Practice by itself is not enough for the youngster: the practice must be relevant; for practice makes **permanent** not perfect. In each chapter of this book and in each section of the video simple practices and games are given for the player and the adult to follow in order to achieve early success.

iv) **Progression**

   ★ To develop effectively children need to want to practice by themselves in their own time: adults should not hesitate to give youngsters soccer 'Homework' - exercises from those recommended that they can do in their own time.

   ★ When the child can display some progress in the technique then practices should involve team mates and defenders, as outlined in this book and on the video.

   ★ Adults must not only insist on a good attitude towards practice but high standards throughout. Knowledge and respect of the Laws of the Game, respect of officials together with good attitudes towards punctuality, appearance, criticism and disappointment are critical factors in the child's development. These standards will be set by the adults' own example, and as a guide a Code of Conduct for the scheme is presented on page 4.

v) **The Award Test**

The programme of instruction should begin with an Assessment test where the scores were merely noted and no awards made.

The course of instruction should be as a minimum 6 hours, to which should be added the Award Test for each technique.

The Award Test is an integral part of learning and should take place at least once every 12 months and at best two or three times a year.

The Award Test should **not** be taken in isolation from the programme of instruction.

vi) **Organising an Award Test**

Ages: The age ranges listed in this book conform to the following deadlines:

UNDER 7 years of age means Under 7 years of age at midnight on the previous 31 August.

UNDER 8 years of age means Under 8 years of age at midnight on the previous 31 August.

UNDER 9 years of age means Under 9 years of age at midnight on the previous 31 August.

UNDER 10 years of age means Under 10 years of age at midnight on the previous 31 August.

UNDER 11 years of age means Under 11 years of age at midnight on the previous 31 August.

UNDER 12 years of age means Under 12 years of age at midnight on the previous 31 August.

UNDER 13 years of age means Under 13 years of age at midnight on the previous 31 August.

UNDER 14 years of age means Under 14 years of age at midnight on the previous 31 August.

UNDER 15 years of age means Under 15 years of age at midnight on the previous 31 August.

UNDER 16 years of age means Under 16 years of age at midnight on the previous 31 August.

Facilities: The tests can be organised inside or outside and on any suitable surface, eg grass, playground, sports hall, synthetic turf, etc.

Equipment:

Soccer balls - 5 required. The appropriate size of ball should be used for the age of the players and the surface used.

Markers/cones - 10 required: please follow the required dimensions precisely. These can be marked out with lines, markers or cones.

Stop Watch - Measuring in 1/10ths of a second. Please record times accurately.

Record Sheet and pencil. Please adhere to the notes on organising each test. You will find them most helpful.

Time: One adult can realistically examine a group of 12 youngsters in an hour and even quicker times will be achieved once the children and the adult have become accustomed to the tests. The tests may be completed all in one session or over a number of sessions.

Recording: It is extremely important to record the correct date of birth as all performance tables are age related. The child's performance should be recorded in the appropriate column. The record sheet should then be sent to the address on the form, together with the required monies.

The course organisers and players will receive, within seven to ten days, reports regarding the achievement and progress of the individual and the class, group or team involved.

These will be in addition to the certificates and badges sent to the player.

This award test performance should therefore act as an assessment test for future periods of instruction, learning and progress as new targets are established.

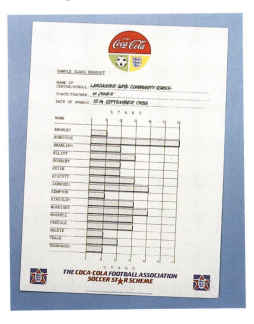

Running with the ball

Running with the ball is the first technique that youngsters learn – they kick and then chase after the ball. Running with the ball is not the same as dribbling. Dribbling involves beating players whereas running with the ball involves moving the ball across areas that do not contain defenders. To be able to cover the ground quickly with the ball under control is a very important and valuable technique.

THE TASK – THE TEST

The purpose of the test is to run the ball as quickly as possible from the starting line until the ball crosses the finishing line.

LET'S SEE YOU DO IT!

ORGANISATION

1 AREA

The area is marked out as shown in the photograph below, with the use of lines or markers.

2 START

The player 'P' begins the test by crossing the line A/B with the ball. The time begins when the ball crosses the line.

3 FINISH

The test finishes when the **ball** crosses the line G/H between the markers G/H no more than 2 feet above ground level. The player may either pass or run the ball over this line. The player must not pass the ball until the ball has passed over the line E/F.

4 TIMING

Time the test to 1/10th of a second from Start to Finish.

5 IF THE PLAYER

 i) passes the ball before the line E/F and does not touch the ball again,

OR

 ii) fails to pass the ball through the finishing line at the required height,

OR

 iii) slips or falls over

then the test should be repeated, up to a maximum of two attempts. If the player has not achieved a score after two attempts, then no score is recorded against the player for this test. Players should be aware that two failures will result in no score being recorded.

HOW QUICKLY CAN YOU RUN WITH THE BALL?

FOR THE COACH/TEACHER/ PARENT/YOUTH LEADER:

ORGANISING A GROUP TO TAKE THE TEST

PLEASE NOTE:

 i) Five balls required.

 ii) Time – 15 players: 10 minutes.

RECORDING

1 Record the times on the Score Sheet under the appropriate column whether Assessment Test or Award Test.

2 On completion of the Test, together with each player, set new targets for the player to strive for when next tested.

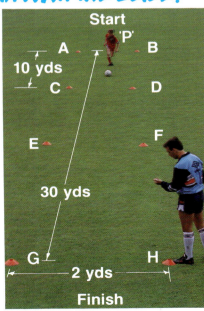

NOW TRY THIS!

How to master the technique and score highly on the test.

STUDY THE VIDEO AND NOTE THE FOLLOWING:

ORGANISATION

A group of 6 players in two groups of three, 40 yards apart. A begins by running the ball before passing to D. A joins the line behind F. D runs the ball, passes to B and joins the line behind C.

DO

1 Make your first touch of the ball well in front of you to allow you to look up. To cover the ground quickly take a few **long** touches. When running with the ball, touch the ball well in front of you to enable you to look up. The more times you touch the ball the slower you will run.

DO

2 Run straight and if possible pass with your laces without interrupting your normal stride. If you have to pass then avoid passing with the side of the foot – this will slow you down.

... with the ball well in front of you progress to this game.

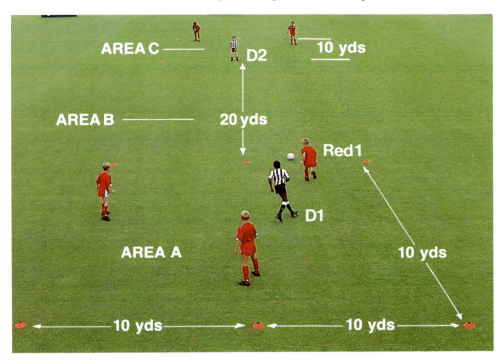

ORGANISATION

AREA: as marked

1   3 Red players begin the practice in Area A by playing against one striped defender **D1** in order to free one Red player into Area B. No Red player can enter area B before the ball arrives there and the defender must stay in area A.

2   For example, the Reds interpass before Red 1 has the space to run the ball through Area B to Area C, where the exercise is repeated in the opposite direction. Likewise no Red player can enter Area B before the ball arrives there and the defender **D2** must stay in Area C.

Change defenders at the appropriate time or when the defenders have forced the Reds into a required number of mistakes.

KEY FACTORS

1   Control the ball in front of you, to be able to run with the ball.

2   Don't pass the ball square when you can run forward with the ball.

3   Run straight through Area B and pass with the laces to maintain momentum.

Turning

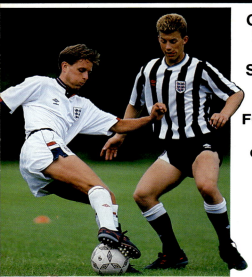

Once you have learnt to run with the ball you will now need to stop, start and change direction with the ball. Soccer is not played in straight lines and whilst soccer is a FORWARD thinking, FORWARD passing, FORWARD running game, sometimes it will be necessary to work the ball out of a crowd of players in order to run or pass the ball forward or have a shot at goal.

It is essential therefore that you are comfortable enough on the ball to be able to turn with the ball and change direction.

THE TASK - THE TEST

The purpose of the test is to complete 9 turns with the ball, as quickly as possible, with three different methods of turning:

LET'S SEE YOU DO IT!

ORGANISATION

The area is marked out as shown in the photograph above.

1 AREA

(a) Two lines are marked five yards apart (A and B).

(b) Two gates are marked five yards apart.

2 START

When the player crosses the start line (A), the examiner starts the clock.

3 TIMING

The player must run the ball over the line B, five yards away between the gates marked. The player must then return to the line A and run the ball **over** the line between the gates marked. The player then returns to run the ball over the line B and returns to cross the line A before putting the foot on the ball to stop the ball. Time to 1/10th of a second.

4 FINISH

The player finishes the attempt of the test by crossing line A and putting the foot on the ball to stop the ball.

5 SCORING

(a) The player will therefore complete **three** turning movements all of which must be the same **movement,** eg:-

i) hooking the ball with the inside of the foot.

ii) hooking the ball with the outside of the foot.

iii) step over turn.

iv) drag back turn.

v) stop/turn.

vi) "Cruyff" turn.

THE Challenge

THE CHALLENGE

The **movement** must therefore be the same but the player can use either right or left foot to execute the movement. Providing the **type** of movement is the same then the player can alternate between right and left feet.

(b) The test is repeated twice more to produce in total three attempts of the test. During the second attempt the player must use a turning movement different to that used in the first attempt. Again, within the second attempt each turn must be the same.

(c) During the third attempt the player must use a turning movement different to that used in the first and second attempts of the test. Again, within the third attempt each turn must be the same.

(d) Add up the three attempts of the test on the score sheet to produce a total time for the test.

(e) The player therefore completes three attempts of the test when, he or she has executed three **different** turning movements on three separate attempts whilst performing the same turning movement within each attempt.

(f) If the player during the test:

i) fails to cross the lines A or B when executing a turn, OR

ii) fails to stop the ball on completion of an attempt beyond the line A, OR

iii) falls, trips or slips over, OR

iv) changes the type of movement on an attempt, OR

v) repeats a type of movement on another attempt.

the player should be re-tested once for **that particular movement** up to a maximum of two attempts for each movement. If the player has not achieved a score after two attempts, then no score is recorded against the player for this movement. Players should be aware of the danger of failing to record a score if they do not concentrate.

HOW QUICKLY CAN YOU TURN WITH THE BALL?

FOR THE COACH/TEACHER/PARENT/YOUTH LEADER: ORGANISING A GROUP TO TAKE THE TEST

PLEASE NOTE:

i) The players should be in pairs, eg A and B. Whilst A makes his/her first attempt B waits: B then makes his/her first attempt whilst A rests. This procedure allows the players to get adequate rest. After A and B have both completed their 3 attempts another pair make their attempts.

ii) The players must demonstrate to the examiner the intended turn before attempting the test. The examiner should be able to identify each method of turning.

iii) Total time for each player to complete three attempts: one minute.

RECORDING

1 Record the times on the Score Sheet under the appropriate column whether Assessment Test or Award Test.

2 On completion of the Test, together with each player, set new targets for the player to strive for when next tested.

NOW TRY THIS!

How to master the technique and score highly on the test.
STUDY THE VIDEO AND NOTE THE FOLLOWING:

★ Watch good players on the Soccer Star Video or at live matches and observe the turns they use. They will perform many of the turns shown here.

★ Practice **all** the turns shown and others you may have seen with both right and left feet but then select only the THREE turns that you are most comfortable with, and MASTER them.

★ The turns shown in the photographs are performed by right-footed players. These should be adapted for left-footed players.

★ Practice these turns as often as possible – in the garden, in the playground, in games – so that YOU take the responsibility for YOUR progress.

★ When practising the turns there are THREE major DOs:
1 Start slowly.
2 Bend your knees.
3 Accelerate away.

---

1 **HOOKING THE BALL WITH THE INSIDE OF THE FOOT**

Reach and Hook to turn the ball....
Don't run around the ball. Move the ball on the turning touch back in the direction you want to go.

2 HOOKING THE BALL WITH THE OUTSIDE OF THE FOOT

Reach and Hook to turn the ball....
Don't run around the ball. Move the
ball on the turning touch well in front
of you, back in the direction you want
to go.

3 THE STEP OVER

Step over the ball low and quickly. Swivel your hips and play the ball back with the inside of your other foot.

4 THE DRAG BACK Turn ball under the body by rolling ball with the sole of the foot.

5   THE STOP/TURN Trap ball under the foot, turn, quickly play the ball with other foot.

6   THE 'CRUYFF' TURN
Turn right foot inward with toe down and push the ball behind and away from you.

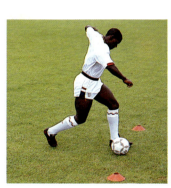

DEVELOPMENT   These practices can be used for all turns

1 'PAIRS'

ORGANISATION   2 players, 10 yards from each other. Two balls required.

DO:

1   Keep your head up to observe the ball and your partner.
2   Turn and accelerate away in the opposite direction, when opposite your partner's shoulders.
3   Keep your body between you and your partner when turning. Use your furthest foot away from your partner. Turn away from him, not in towards him.

2 'TAG'

ORGANISATION

AREA: 10yds x 10yds

Both players have a ball. One defending player – in stripes – has to keep the ball under control and tag the White player who attempts to avoid the striped player by turning with the ball. Play for 30 seconds and count how many times the defender can tag the White player. Both players must keep the ball within the area. If the ball goes out of the area a 'tag' is awarded to the other player.

Change places after 30 seconds so that White then chases the striped player.

DO:

1   Play with your head up to see where your partner is.
2   Practice your three best turns.
3   Turn and accelerate away.

STREETGAMES

Be a star – show off and show us a turn!

'THREES' When you can use your three turns effectively then play the following games with opposition.

1 Red passes the ball to White 10 yards away and follows the pass to attempt to get the ball from White.

White lets the ball run and controls the ball away from Red with his back to Red.

2 White with his back to Red shields the ball from Red and when Red is attempting to win the ball by challenging on one side of White, White turns the other way by executing one of his three best turns.

3 White then passes to Blue 10 yards away and follows his pass to challenge Blue. Blue must then complete a turn and pass to Red. The practice then continues.

DO: 1 Shield the ball – keep your body between the ball and the defender.
2 When the defender challenges on one side – turn the other way.
3 Accelerate away.

'2 v 2'
ORGANISATION AREA: 20 yds x 20 yds
2 White players play against 2 striped defenders.

The White players receive the ball from a Red player outside the area and must pass the ball to either of the Red target players outside the area. The White players can in turn pass to their team-mate or pass back to the Red player outside the area who started the game.

The striped defenders try to gain possession and pass the ball to one of the Red players outside the area. The practice continues with either team in possession for three minutes and then two of the players inside the area change with the Red players.

DO
1 Spread out to allow the player on the ball space to turn against his/her opponent.
2 Disguise your intentions when on the ball. Pretend to pass and then turn. Pretend to turn and then pass.
3 Shield the ball and play with your head up.

DON'T
1 Bunch so that both defenders are near the ball.
2 Pass to the team mate inside the area when there is an opportunity to turn and pass the ball to the target player outside the area.

DON'T pass for the sake of it – DO take responsibility and attempt a turn.

Speed

We have seen from the previous section how important it is to be able to change speed and accelerate away from defenders. In soccer you are required not only to run quickly but also stop, start and change direction.

These abilities can be improved so that the 'speed' test is really a test of how quickly you can change direction and change speed.

THE CHALLENGE

THE TASK – THE TEST
The purpose of the test is to run as quickly as possible AROUND the markers from start to finish.

LET'S SEE YOU DO IT!

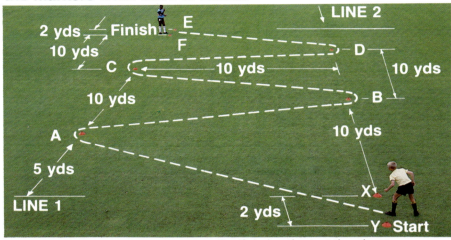

TEST

1. The area is laid out as shown in the photograph above.
2. The player starts behind the line between the starting cones/markers (X/Y).
3. No ball is required – this is a test for speed and mobility.
4. On the command 'ready – go' the player runs **around** the cones/markers A, B, C, D to finish across the line between cones E and F.
5. Time the test to 1/10th of a second from start to finish.
6. If during the test the player:
   i) fails to run around any of the cones, OR
   ii) falls, trips or slips over

   then the player should be re-tested. If **either** of these situations i) to ii) above occur, the player should be re-tested once, up to a maximum of two attempts. If the player has not achieved a score after two attempts, then no score is recorded against the player for this test. Re-test players should go to the end of the line to allow a maximum rest period.

HOW QUICKLY CAN YOU RUN THE COURSE?

FOR THE COACH/TEACHER/PARENT/YOUTH LEADER: ORGANISING A GROUP TO TAKE THE TEST
i) The test is completed very quickly with total time for testing 10-15 players less than 5 minutes.

RECORDING
i) Record the times on the Score Sheet under the appropriate column whether Assessment Test or Award Test.
ii) On completion of the Test, together with each player, set new targets for the player to strive for when next tested.

NOW TRY THIS!

How to master the technique and score highly on the test.
STUDY THE VIDEO AND NOTE THE FOLLOWING:
There are two key factors to learn to score highly on the test.

1. How to keep your body – your centre of gravity – low in order to turn quickly. To do this it is necessary for you to bend your knees and lean forward when changing direction.
2. How to accelerate quickly away from the turns. To do this you should follow this advice:
   ★ keep your head still (don't shake it from side to side).
   ★ lift your knees when running.
   ★ swing your arms backwards and forwards not across your body.

Here are some simple practices to help you.

BEND THOSE KNEES!

1 'FAKE AND DODGE'

ORGANISATION
★ A Line 10 yds wide.
★ 4 markers A B C D.
★ The striped defender chases the Yellow attacker.
★ The Yellow player must touch yellow markers A or B before the defender can touch the nearest red markers C or D respectively.
★ After three attempts the players change places.

KEY FACTORS
★ Wrong foot the defender
★ Lean forward
★ Bend your knees

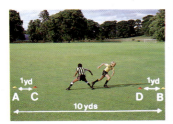

2 'NORTH AND SOUTH'

ORGANISATION
★ Area 10 yds x 10 yds square.
★ Two sides of the square are labelled 'North' and 'South'.
★ Two players lie down side by side – head to toe – in the middle of the area.
★ One of them acts as the 'caller' to shout 'North' or 'South' and on this command they must get up quickly and race for the 'North' or 'South' line.
★ The first over the nominated line wins and the loser acts as the caller for the next race.

KEY FACTORS
★ Get up into a position to run as quickly as possible – keep low. Don't stand up straight and then run, but start running for the line in as low a position as soon as possible.
★ Lead your momentum with your head – but keep it steady.

4 'HOPPING AND SKIPPING'

Hopping and skipping will help you develop strength in your leg muscles so attempt the following practices:
With a friend: Hopping races 10 yards one way on your right foot and 10 yards back on your left foot.
By yourself: Skipping – with a skipping rope.

5 Finally try attempting the test as often as possible to improve your ability and measure your progress. Give yourself 3-5 minutes rest in between attempts.

3 'SPRINTS'

ORGANISATION
★ The Yellow player stands on the line X/Y facing the striped player who is standing behind the line A/B.
★ The line A/B is 2 yards from the line X/Y.
★ The striped player decides when to start to run to attempt to cross the finishing line C/D first.
★ As soon as the striped player begins to run the Yellow player must turn and also attempt to finish first across the finishing line.
★ The Yellow player cannot turn until the striped player begins to run.
★ Change positions on the next attempt.

KEY FACTORS
★ For the Yellow player: Lean into the turn with your head first and bend your knees to turn quickly.
★ For both players: To run quickly – keep your head still and steady. Lift your knees.

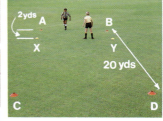

Dribbling

Dribbling is one of soccer's most effective and exciting techniques. Here are three simple rules to remember.

1 WHERE TO DRIBBLE?

Dribbling involves risk so DON'T dribble in or around your own penalty area, but DO dribble in or around your opponent's penalty area.

2 WHEN TO DRIBBLE

DO be prepared to dribble as often as possible. Even the best dribblers fail more often than they succeed.

DON'T be afraid to have a go!

3 WHY?

Good dribblers dribble for a purpose – to create space to shoot at goal or pass to a colleague to shoot at goal.

So...

DO get maximum benefit from your dribble.

DON'T waste the chance to shoot or pass to a team-mate who can.

THE TASK – THE TEST

Imagine the markers are defenders and the purpose of the test is to dribble the ball as quickly as possible in front and away from the markers, A B C D from the start of the course to the finish.

LET'S SEE YOU DO IT!

AREA: The area is marked out as shown in the photograph on page 24 with lines, cones or markers.

1. The player stands with one foot on the ball behind the starting line.
2. The time begins when the player crosses the starting line.
3. The ball must:
   i) cross the line 1 **in front of** the cones/markers at A and C.
   ii) cross the line 2 **in front of** the cones/markers at B and D.
   iii) **not** touch the cones/markers (the players are allowed to touch the cones/markers with their feet).
4. The player must:
   i) dribble **in front of** the cones/markers A, B, C and D,
   ii) stop the ball **beyond** the finishing line between the two cones/markers (E and F) indicating the finishing gate.
5. The test ends with the player with one foot on the ball past the finishing line between the width of the finishing gate markers.
6. **Time** the dribbling test to 1/10th of a second from start to finish.
7. If the whole of the ball during the test:
   i) fails to **cross** the line **in front of** any of the marker cones (A, B, C, D), OR
   If the player during the test:
   ii) dribbles **behind** any of the marker cones (A, B, C, D) or the cones marking the finishing gate, OR
   iii) dribbles the ball to touch any of the marker cones (A, B, C, D) or the cones marking the finishing gate, OR
   iv) fails to stop the ball beyond the finishing line, OR
   v) falls, trips or slips over
   then the player should be re-tested. If **any** of the situations i) to v) above occur, the player should be re-tested once, up to a maximum of two attempts. If the player has not achieved a score after two attempts, then no score is recorded against the player for this test. Re-test players should go to the end of the line to allow a maximum rest period.

   Players need to concentrate and be aware of the possibility of failing to record a score if they do not concentrate.

FOR THE COACH/TEACHER/PARENT/YOUTH LEADER:

ORGANISING A GROUP TO TAKE THE TEST
See photograph below of a group being tested.
ii) 1 is being tested.
ii) 2 – 7 are waiting to be tested.
iii) 8 and 9 are 'spotters' to ensure the ball of the player being tested crosses the line.
iv) 10 collects the ball.
v) Time: one minute per player.
vi) 3 balls required.
vii) It is advisable to use cones for A B C and D. They can be more easily seen by the player than markers.
viii) Emphasize to the players that the cones should be looked upon as 'stationary' defenders – therefore change direction in front of them.

RECORDING

1. Record the scores on the score sheet under the appropriate column whether Assessment or Award Test.
2. On completion of the Test together with each player, set new targets for the players to strive for when next tested.

HOW QUICKLY CAN YOU DRIBBLE?

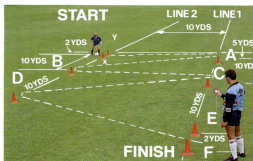

NOW TRY THIS!

How to master the technique and score highly on the test.
STUDY THE VIDEO AND NOTE THE FOLLOWING:

You can use any move you wish in order to complete the test, but to achieve the best results from this test and to develop your dribbling you should:

1. Imagine that the markers are defenders.
2. Use a 'fake' or a 'feint' in front of the markers – pretend to go outside but pass the marker on the inside.
3. Accelerate away from the marker.
4. When learning the moves begin **slowly.**

The moves listed will help you make progress in your dribbling technique. Try these moves and others you may know but to assist you, select one move to use when passing markers A and C on Line 1 and one move to use when passing markers B and D on Line 2.

The three moves are described and illustrated for right footed players. These can and should, of course, be adapted and practised by all players on their left side.

THE MOVES
1 'MATTHEWS'

1. Move the ball with the **inside** of your right foot to your left side and fake to go to your left, by leaning to the left.
2. Move your right foot quickly behind the ball so that the **outside** of your right foot is behind the ball.
3. Accelerate away to your right using the outside of your right foot to push the ball forward and **past** the marker.

2 'SCISSORS'

1. Play the ball out in front of your right side.
2. Pretend to play the ball with the outside of the right foot but step over the ball with your right foot.
3. Take the ball away with the outside of your left foot past the marker.

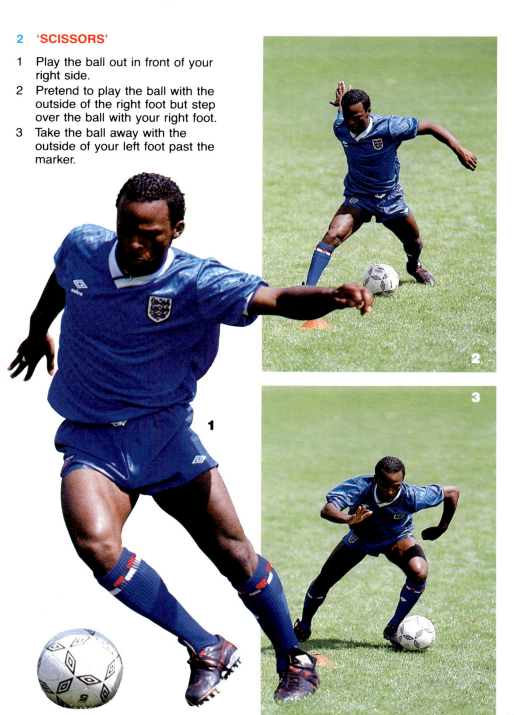

3 'DOUBLE TOUCH'

1. Pretend to be about to play the ball to your right with the inside of your right foot – your upper body should be at an angle.
2. Draw the ball across the body with the inside of your right foot.
3. Take the ball away to your left side with the inside of your left foot past the marker.

If you are prepared to be POSITIVE and AGGRESSIVE on the ball progress to the following games:

1 '4 MARKERS'

ORGANISATION

AREA: 10 YDS x 20 YDS markers A, B, C, D

RULES:

1. The striped defender starts the practice by passing to the Blue attacker.
2. The Blue player's target is to kick the ball against any of the four markers (A, B, C, D).
3. The Blue player must keep the ball inside the area.
4. The striped player may challenge anywhere for the ball once the Blue player has received it.
5. If the Blue player goes into area 2 he/she cannot attack markers A or B.
6. Players change places after three attempts.

KEY FACTORS

★ Be positive from the moment you control the ball. Control the ball in front of you and attack the space either side of the defender on your first touch.

★ Attack with the ball in the direction of one of the markers.

★ Commit the defender to going one way and then use one of your favourite moves to wrong-foot him/her to accelerate the other way.

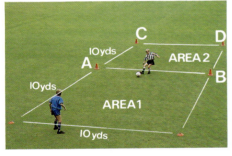

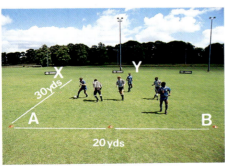

2 '3 v 3'

ORGANISATION

★ Area 30 yds x 20 yds.

★ To score, one team must dribble the ball across the line which is behind the defenders (A/B or X/Y).

★ The team scoring keeps possession and plays in the opposite direction.

KEY FACTORS

Dribble when:

1. Space is available.
2. You are not outnumbered by defenders.

31

Heading

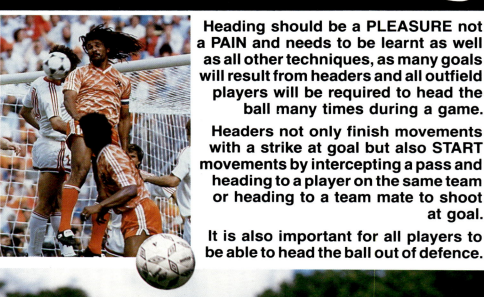

Heading should be a PLEASURE not a PAIN and needs to be learnt as well as all other techniques, as many goals will result from headers and all outfield players will be required to head the ball many times during a game.

Headers not only finish movements with a strike at goal but also START movements by intercepting a pass and heading to a player on the same team or heading to a team mate to shoot at goal.

It is also important for all players to be able to head the ball out of defence.

THE TASK – THE TEST
The purpose of the test is to head the ball over the goal line into the goal with, at the most, only one bounce.

LET'S SEE YOU DO IT!

ORGANISATION

1. The **area** is marked out with the use of a goal, goal line, and markers or cones as shown in the photographs opposite. The goal should be standard (8 yards x 8 feet). Posts, cones or markers may be used instead of a goal but must be placed 8 yards apart: the examiner would then need to judge whether a header would have entered the goal below the crossbar had it been there.

2. The **player** – 'P' stands behind the line C/D.

3. The **server 'S'** – stands behind the line X/Y with a ball and throws the ball – two handed – using an under arm serve at around head height so that if the ball came to ground it would land between the line A/B and the line C/D. The quality of service is crucial: the examiner should serve to enable 'P' to have the **best** possible service to score. If the service is not to the satisfaction of the examiner then the service should be repeated.

4. To **score:**
★ 'P' judges the service, moves forward to head the ball and makes contact before the line A/B.
★ If 'P' first makes contact with the ball after crossing the line A/B then that header cannot score. The ball may go straight into the goal without bouncing on the ground or it may bounce **once** on the ground before crossing the line. The ball to score must **not** bounce twice on the ground before crossing the goal line.

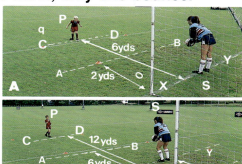

5. **Attempts:**
'P' Receives – 3 serves
The examiner to record each goal as one point and failure to score as 0 (zero). Total up at the end of the test.

6. If the ball:
i) bounces twice on the ground before crossing the goal line – no score.
ii) hits the crossbar, one or both posts and crosses the goal line without bouncing twice on the ground – score one point.
iii) hits the crossbar, one or both posts, bounces twice on the ground and crosses the goal line – no score.

7. **Changes for ages:**
As shown on the photographs above.
A - Under 9's
B - Under 11's
C - Over 11's e.g. Under 12's, 13's, 14's, 15's, and 16's.

HOW MANY GOALS CAN YOU SCORE?

FOR THE COACH/TEACHER/PARENT/YOUTH LEADER:
ORGANISING A GROUP TO TAKE THE TEST
Please note:

i) 1 – being tested
    2/3/4/5/6 – waiting to be tested
    7 – recording marks; constant for 11 players. Number 7 is tested last.
    8/9 – supplying examiner with balls.
    10/11/12 – 'retrievers'; give balls to 8 or 9.

ii) Numbers 1 – 6 have one attempt then go to the back of the line until all six have had three attempts. Numbers 1 – 6 then change with numbers 8 – 12. Number 7 is tested last.

RECORDING

1 Record the scores on the score sheet under the appropriate column whether Assessment Test or Award Test.

2 On completion of the Test together with each player set new targets for the player to strive for when next tested.

NOW TRY THIS!
How to master the technique and score highly on the test.

STUDY THE VIDEO AND NOTE THE FOLLOWING:

Start by throwing the ball on to your head to head to a partner 5 yards away.

DO

1 Attack the ball: feet apart, withdraw head and arch body; arms back and neck firm.

2 Use the centre of the forehead and try to look through the ball. Your eyes will close briefly on impact with the ball, but don't close them before heading the ball.

3 Head **through** the ball
   The ball will not hurt if you attack the ball rather than the ball attacking you!

Don't begin heading with a ball thrown at you by someone else. Begin by throwing the ball on to your head.

Don't head the ball with the top of your head.

Don't close your eyes

Do keep your eyes open

Do use your forehead

If you're prepared to ATTACK the ball then head for success.

1 'HEADERS'

ORGANISATION

The area is a 10 yards long with goals 4 yards apart.
The Maroon player throws the ball up and attempts to head past the striped player to score in the goal under head height.
The striped player saves using his/her hands and repeats the attempt to score past the Maroon player.
Either player instead of using their hands to save can attempt a return header to score back against the opponent.
Return headers score 2 goals.

KEY FACTORS

★ Don't be afraid to head the ball back.
★ Head through the ball.
★ Diving headers are very important in keeping the ball low.

2 'OVER/UNDER'

ORGANISATION

★ The Maroon player stands 10 yards away from the striped player who has his/her legs apart and throws the ball for the Maroon player to head back.
★ The striped player shouts either 'over' or 'under'.
★ To score: For 'under' the Maroon player must head the ball through the striped player's legs.
★ For 'over' the Maroon player must head the ball over the striped player's head.

KEY FACTORS

★ Head through the top half of the ball to head down.
★ Head through the bottom half of the ball to head up.

OVER UNDER

STREETGAMES

'PAIRED HEADERS'

As for 'Headers' on page 35 but 2 Maroon players play against 2 striped players.

Goal 8 yards apart. A throws to B to attempt to head past C and D under head height into the goal.

'Return' headers score 2 goals.

KEY FACTORS

To angle the header from B, A must:-
★ get on line with the ball.
★ rotate the head on contact with the ball, towards the goal.
★ not attempt to angle the header by using the side of the head.

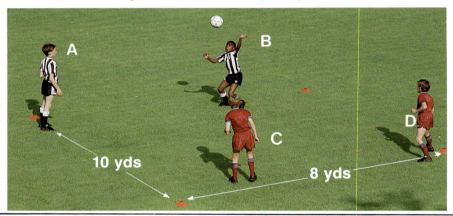

'THROW/HEAD/CATCH'

ORGANISATION

Area: 40 yds x 30 yds
Goals: 8 yds apart
Teams: 6 v 6 (no goalkeepers)
Scoring: Only headed goals can score

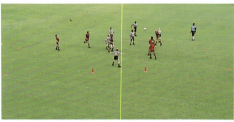

Rules:
1 The team in possession can only make progress by using the throw/head/catch sequence. No player is allowed to run with the ball whilst in possession.
2 The opposition can only gain possession by intercepting using a header from an opposition throw or a catch from an opposition header.
3 There are no goalkeepers. The ball may bounce, but if it rolls along the ground it becomes dead and the other team gains possession.
4 Throw the ball in for both corners and throw-ins.

Shooting

The object of soccer is to score goals: shooting is therefore obviously vital. All other soccer techniques are wasted if shooting chances are not taken – therefore, take each and every shooting opportunity that occurs.

One aspect is certain: you may not score everytime you shoot BUT YOU WILL NOT SCORE UNLESS YOU SHOOT. Be sure to take your responsibility to shoot, score and...sometimes miss.

Records have shown that a high percentage of shots are taken not directly in front of goal but from an angle to the side of the goal.

Not surprisingly, defenders will defend the area immediately in front of the goal, so more of the chances to shoot are presented to the side of goals. Shooting practice should therefore be concentrated on angled shots.

It is important wherever possible to practice shooting in full-size goals: where this is not possible the goal should be at least the correct width even if cones, corner posts or even coats are used.

When shooting it is important to understand two key aspects.

★ LOW OR HIGH SHOTS?

Low shots are harder for the goalkeeper to save. High shots allow the goalkeeper to pick up the flight of the ball and shorter distances to move to save them.

Low shots can be deflected into goal by another player: high shots going over the bar therefore cannot be deflected.

Low shots can also cause problems for the goalkeeper by bumping or skidding on the surface: high shots cannot.

Low shots are best achieved by striking through the middle of the ball with the laces.

Whatever you do therefore go for accuracy before power and do not miss by shooting over the crossbar – it is less of a sin to shoot wide rather than high.

★ NEAR OR FAR HALF OF THE GOAL?

Shots going away from the goalkeeper are harder for the goalkeeper to save than shots towards the near half of the goal. Shots going away from the goalkeeper are also harder for the goalkeeper to hold and, as such, present rebounds for team mates to score.

If the Attacker in photograph (a) shoots for the near half of the goal and the goalkeeper deflects the ball - a corner results. If the Attacker in photograph (b) shoots for the far half of the goal and the goalkeeper deflects the ball this will be across the goal and present an opportunity for a team-mate to score. Shots to the far half of the goal therefore have a greater chance of producing secondary scoring opportunities.

Furthermore if you consistently aim for the far half of the goal and miss this target, your shot will at worst go for goal or miss at the far post: if you aim for the near half of the goal and miss, your shot will miss the goal at the near post and produce no secondary scoring opportunities.

Accuracy in shooting is more important than power.

Therefore if you are going to miss -

**Don't miss over the bar
Don't miss at the near post
but, if you have to miss – miss just beyond the far post.**

THE TASK - THE TEST

The purpose of the test is to gain the highest number of points by aiming to shoot the ball into the half of the goal furthest away from the player shooting.

LET'S SEE YOU DO IT!

ORGANISATION
AREA: The area is shown in the photograph below.

1. A goal 8 yards wide and 8 feet high without a goal net, with two cones each three yards from each post and a corner flag/cone in the middle of the goal.

   Two power lines are either marked, or signified by markers/cones: power line (a) is 5 yards behind the goal line and power line (b) is 10 yards behind the goal.

2. The player stands with a ball 18 yards from the goal and level with the cone at the near post.

   The player touches the ball into the penalty area (but no more than three yards forward) and then on the second touch, **whilst the ball is in motion**, shoots for goal. The ball must be moving when struck. If this is not the case, the player should be re-tested, up to a maximum of two attempts. If the player has not achieved a score after two serves, then no score is recorded against the player for this attempt.

3. The ball must be struck in a 'shooting' action, ie with the laces. A 'push' pass with the side of the foot is not permitted nor is a 'toe poke' with the toe. If a push pass with the side of the foot or a toe poke is taken this attempt must be repeated up to a maximum of two serves. If the player has not achieved an attempt after two serves, then no score is recorded against the player for this attempt.

4. If the player touches the ball more than three yards the attempt must be repeated up to a maximum of two attempts. If the player has not achieved a score after two serves, then no score is recorded against the player for this attempt.

SCORING

5. The following points are scored:
   i) 3 points for the shot crossing the goal line at any height, including ground level, and entering the goal between the far post and centre goal marker.
   ii) 1 point for the shot that passes between the far post and the far post marker below the height of the crossbar.
   iii) 2 points for the shot that passes into the goal between the near post and centre goal marker.
   iv) 0 points are scored if the shot misses over the bar or at the near post.

6. Three attempts are made from the right side and three attempts are made from the left side. The attempts from the right side must be made with the right foot and attempts from the left side with the left foot. If an attempt is made with the wrong foot this attempt cannot score and no points are awarded for this attempt.

7. If the ball hits the **crossbar**
   – and goes over the bar: score 0 points.
   – and rebounds into the penalty area: score 0 points.
   – and goes into the goal: score 2 or 3 points depending on which area of the goal, the ball crosses the line to enter the goal.

8. If the ball hits the **near post**
   – and goes wide of the goal at the near post: score 0 points.
   – and goes into the goal: score 2 or 3 points depending on which area of the goal, the ball crossed the line.
   – and goes wide of the goal at the far post: score 0 points.
   – and goes over the bar: score 0 points.

9. If the ball hits the **far post**
   – and goes into the goal: score 2 or 3 points depending on the area in which the ball first crosses the line.

10. If the ball hits the far post and rebounds into the penalty area, or rebounds wide of the goal at the far or near post, or goes over the crossbar: score 1 point.

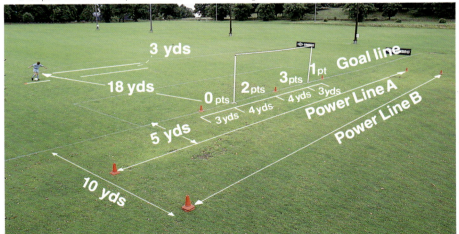

THE CHALLENGE

HOW MANY POINTS CAN YOU SCORE?

The test remains unchanged for players under 7, 8 and 9 years of age.
The 'Power Lines' do not therefore refer to players under 7, 8 and 9 years of age.

CHANGES FOR AGES

1. For players under 10 and 11 years of age, the test has the following modifications:

   To score 1, 2 or 3 points, the pass must cross the 5 yard 'power' line behind the goal line. If the ball crosses the goal line but fails to cross the 5 yard 'power' line, then no points are scored.

2. For players aged under 12 years of age and above, the test has the following modifications:

   To score 1, 2 or 3 points, the ball must cross the 10 yard 'power' line behind the goal line. If the ball crosses the goal line but fails to cross the 10 yard 'power' line, then no points are scored.

FOR THE COACH/TEACHER/PARENT/YOUTH LEADER: ORGANISING A GROUP TO TAKE THE TEST

See photograph below of a group being tested.

PLEASE NOTE:

i) Test all on right foot, then all on left foot. Balls relayed in the same direction as foot, ie test right foot; passed to the right and test left foot; passed to the left.

   Use only 5 balls otherwise a 'shooting gallery' results.

iii) If testing 15 players allow for more players in the 'chain'.

iv) Time: 1 minute for right foot; one minute for left foot. One minute to re-organise. Total time: 3 minutes for each player.

v) Examiners should use their discretion where tests are taking place in either a Sports Hall or where there is insufficient clearance behind the goals for a 'Power' line. In these circumstances, the examiner can judge whether the ball was struck sufficiently hard enough that in the examiner's opinion it would have crossed over the power lines had they been there.

vi) Wherever possible use full-size goals but if this proves difficult to organise then use markers, cones or corner flags, 8 yards apart: the examiner would then decide whether a ball would have gone over the crossbar had it been there.

RECORDING

1. Record the points on the score sheet under the appropriate column whether Assessment or Award Test.

2. On completion of the Test together with each player set new targets for the player to strive for when next tested.

NOW TRY THIS!

How to master the technique and score highly in the test.
STUDY THE VIDEO AND NOTE THE FOLLOWING:

DO

KEEP THE BALL LOW
- ★ Place your non-kicking foot beside the ball. Keep your head still and head over the ball.
- ★ Keep your ankle extended and hit the ball with the laces.
- ★ Be sure to make contact through the middle of the ball.

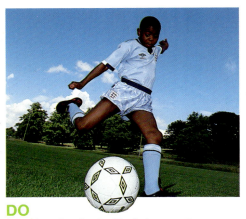

DON'T - WRONG

MISS OVER THE BAR

DON'T STRETCH TO SHOOT
DON'T BRING YOUR HEAD UP TO LOOK UP
DON'T MAKE CONTACT UNDERNEATH THE BALL
All these will make the ball rise.
Make sure to keep it low.

DO

Aim for the far half of the goal away from the goalkeeper.

For right-footed shots:

★ Point your left shoulder and left foot at the far half of the goal.
★ Follow through in the direction of the far corner.
★ Hit through the middle of the ball.
★ Keep your head still and down even after the ball has been struck.

DON'T - WRONG

DON'T MISS AT THE NEAR POST

Don't point your non-kicking foot at the near post – point it towards the far half of the goal.

Don't point your left shoulder towards the near post – point it towards the far half of the goal.

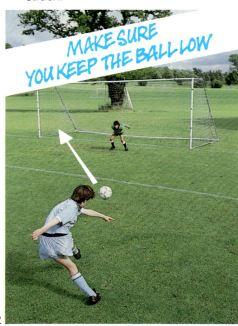

MAKE SURE YOU KEEP THE BALL LOW

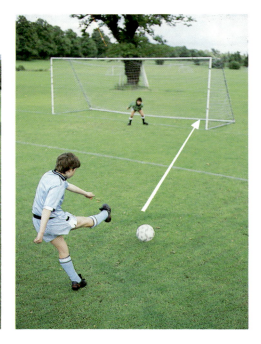

STREETGAMES

'3 and IN'

ORGANISATION

★ The goalkeeper kicks or throws the ball out of goal into space. The Blue and striped players challenge for the ball. Whoever gains possession attacks; the other player becomes the defender.

★ The first player to get 3 goals stays as the Attacker; the loser and goalkeeper change.

KEY FACTORS

★ Take each and every opportunity to shoot.
★ You do not need to dribble past the defender to shoot. Can you shoot the ball past or around the defender?

'2 v 2'

ORGANISATION

★ The goalkeeper distributes the ball into space but now it's 2 Blue players – v – 2 striped players.
★ First team to score 3 goals wins

KEY FACTORS

★ Take your opportunities to shoot.
★ Aim for the far half of the goal.
★ Keep the ball low.
★ Follow in **all** shots for rebounds.

Passing & Control

If you attempt these tests, enjoy the practices listed and play the street games with your friends – in the schoolyard or on the recreation ground – you will as a result get lots of practice of passing and controlling the ball. The practices on turning, dribbling and running with the ball will help improve your 'touch' and the shooting activities will help you pass accurately over varying distances.

Both passing and control are dynamic skills best developed in small game situations but, nevertheless, listed below are some simple exercises to improve controlling and passing the ball.

ORGANISATION

The players pass the ball either side of each other. The players are allowed two touches – one touch to control the ball and one to pass the ball. The conditions can then change to any of the following:

1. Control with one foot: pass with the same foot.
2. Control with one foot; pass with the other foot.
3. Control with the outside of one foot and pass with the inside of the same foot.
4. Control with the inside of one foot and pass with the outside of the same foot.

DO:
- ★ Get in line with the ball.
- ★ Select the surface to control the ball.
- ★ Keep your head still.
- ★ Withdraw and relax the controlling surface to cushion the ball off to the side to create a new angle to pass the ball.

When passing **DO:**
- ★ Place the non-kicking foot as near the ball as possible.
- ★ Kick through the middle of the ball with a firm foot.
- ★ Keep your head still.
- ★ Follow through in the direction you want the ball to go.

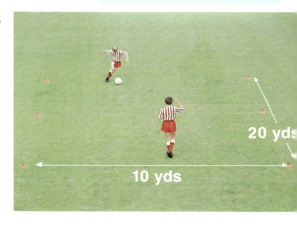

'4 v 2'
ORGANISATION

★ 4 Red striped players against 2 striped defenders in the area 20 yds x 20 yds.

★ The attackers attempt to score a goal by passing the ball (below head height) **between** the defenders.

★ The defenders score if they gain possession of the ball OR force the attackers to pass the ball out of the area.

★ Change places after three minutes.

DO:

1 Look to control the ball to be able to pass the ball forward between the two defenders.

2 Pass the ball as **early** and as **accurately** as often as possible between the defenders.

3 Be able to disguise your control and pass. Pretend to control the ball in one direction but control the ball in a different direction. Fake to pass to your left but pass to your right and vice-versa.

For further development of passing and control, please look at the next section on Small-sided games.

Small-sided Games

FOR THE COACH/TEACHER/PARENT/YOUTH LEADER

SMALL-SIDED GAMES

For the techniques covered, the development has culminated in street games or small-sided games of 3 v 3, 4 v 4, 5 v 5, 6 v 6. These games have been the basis of many great players' development: games that have taken place in the street, the schoolyard, the playground or on the beach have four main advantages over eleven-a-side soccer for youngsters.

1. Each player will have more ball contact and as such will have increased opportunity to develop their techniques.
2. The ball is never far away from the player and therefore concentration is increased.
3. Small-sided games will develop better fitness and awareness without the tactical regimentation often seen in 11 v 11 soccer.
4. Small-sided games are simple to understand, organise and more fun to play!

Therefore all coaches, teachers, parents and youth leaders involved with youngsters are implored to play **small**-sided games at least until the youngsters are 10 or 11 years of age.

Here are two recommended small-sided games:

1 '3 v 3'

Area: 30 yds x 20 yds
Goals: 6 yds wide
Rules:

1. The team defending must have one player back in goal as the goalkeeper.
2. If the ball goes out – pass it in.
3. No offside.

2 '6 v 6'

Area: 50 yds x 30 yds
Goals: 6 yds wide
Rules:

1. Normal soccer with throw-ins, corners and goal kicks.
2. Offside is played.

Simple Key Factors for the young player and the Adult to observe in small-sided games.

When Attacking:

1. Players should spread out to receive the ball – eg stand between and away from defenders.
2. For the player in possession –
   can I shoot?
   can I dribble and shoot?
   can I pass to someone who can?
3. After passing the ball – move again to receive the ball – 'Pass and move'.

When Defending:

1. Stop the player on the ball passing, running or dribbling the ball forward.
2. Stay on your feet! – Do not make clumsy, lunging challenges.

UNDER 7'S

BE SURE TO CHECK THE CORRECT TABLE FOR YOUR AGE

HOW WELL DID YOU DO?

1 WRITE DOWN YOUR TEST RESULTS IN THIS TABLE. RECORD THE TIMED TESTS TO 1/10th OF A SECOND.

		RUNNING WITH THE BALL (Secs)	TURNING (Secs)	SPEED (Secs)	DRIBBLING (Secs)	HEADING	SHOOTING	TOTALS
1st Attempt	Score							
	Pts							
2nd Attempt	Score							
	Pts							
3rd Attempt	Score							
	Pts							
4th Attempt	Score							
	Pts							

Running with the ball		Turning		Speed		Dribbling		Heading		Shooting	
Time (secs)	Points	Time (secs)	Points	Time (secs)	Points	Time (secs)	Points	Goals	Points	Score	Points
under 5.8	5	under 31	15	under 13.5	5	under 19	15	3	5	16 & above	10
5.8 – 6.2	4	31.0 – 32.9	12	13.5 – 14.5	4	19.0 – 20.9	12	2	3	14 – 15	8
6.3 – 7.3	3	33.0 – 37.9	9	14.6 – 15.8	3	21.0 – 22.9	9	1	2	10 – 13	6
7.4 – 8.4	2	38.0 – 42.9	6	15.9 – 17.1	2	23.0 – 26.9	6	0	1	7 – 9	4
8.5 & over	1	43 & over	3	17.2 & over	1	27 & over	3			under 7	2

STAR TABLE

Total Points	Stars
45 & over	Champion Class
37 – 44	5
30 – 36	4
18 – 29	3
14 – 17	2
Under 14	1

2 For each test look up the points table to see how many points you have scored. For example, if you took 37.9 seconds on Test 2 (Turning) then this falls between 33 and 38 seconds and you would earn 9 points.

3 Write down your points in the table against each test.

4 Add up your points to get a Total.

5 Look up the Star Table to see how many stars you have gained (for example, if you scored 29 points you would have achieved a 3 ★★★ grade).

6 Record your Star Grade on page 65.

7 Set yourself a target to achieve the next time you are tested.

HOW WELL DID YOU DO?

1. WRITE DOWN YOUR TEST RESULTS IN THIS TABLE.
   RECORD THE TIMED TESTS TO 1/10th OF A SECOND.

BE SURE TO CHECK THE CORRECT TABLE FOR YOUR AGE

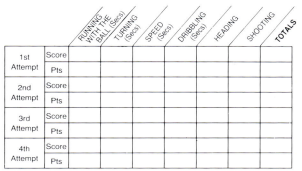

		Running with the ball (Secs)	Turning (Secs)	Speed (Secs)	Dribbling (Secs)	Heading	Shooting	TOTALS
1st Attempt	Score							
	Pts							
2nd Attempt	Score							
	Pts							
3rd Attempt	Score							
	Pts							
4th Attempt	Score							
	Pts							

Running with the ball		Turning		Speed		Dribbling		Heading		Shooting	
Time (secs)	Points	Time (secs)	Points	Time (secs)	Points	Time (secs)	Points	Goals	Points	Score	Points
under 5.3	5	under 30	15	under 13.3	5	under 18	15	3	5	16 & over	10
5.3 – 5.6	4	30.0 – 31.9	12	13.3 – 14.1	4	18.0 – 19.9	12	2	3	14 – 15	8
5.7 – 6.7	3	32.0 – 36.9	9	14.2 – 15.4	3	20.0 – 21.9	9	1	2	10 – 13	6
6.8 – 7.7	2	37.0 – 40.9	6	15.5 – 16.7	2	22.0 – 25.9	6	0	1	8 – 9	4
7.8 & over	1	41 & over	3	16.8 & over	1	26 & over	3			under 8	2

STAR TABLE

Total Points	Stars
46 & over	Champion Class
37 – 45	5
30 – 36	4
20 – 29	3
16 – 19	2
Under 16	1

2. For each test look up the points table to see how many points you have scored. For example, if you took 36.9 seconds on Test 2 (Turning) then this falls between 32 and 37 seconds and you would earn 9 points.
3. Write down your points in the table against each test.
4. Add up your points to get a Total.
5. Look up the Star Table to see how many stars you have gained (for example, if you scored 29 points you would have achieved a 3 ★★★ grade).
6. Record your Star Grade on page 65.
7. Set yourself a target to achieve the next time you are tested.

UNDER 9'S

BE SURE TO CHECK THE CORRECT TABLE FOR YOUR AGE

HOW WELL DID YOU DO?

1 WRITE DOWN YOUR TEST RESULTS IN THIS TABLE. RECORD THE TIMED TESTS TO 1/10th OF A SECOND.

		RUNNING WITH THE BALL (Secs)	TURNING (Secs)	SPEED (Secs)	DRIBBLING (Secs)	HEADING	SHOOTING	TOTALS
1st Attempt	Score							
	Pts							
2nd Attempt	Score							
	Pts							
3rd Attempt	Score							
	Pts							
4th Attempt	Score							
	Pts							

Running with the ball		Turning		Speed		Dribbling		Heading		Shooting	
Time (secs)	Points	Time (secs)	Points	Time (secs)	Points	Time (secs)	Points	Goals	Points	Score	Points
under 4.9	5	under 29	15	under 13.1	5	under 17	15	3	5	16 & above	10
4.9 – 5.2	4	29.0 – 30.9	12	13.1 – 13.7	4	17.0 – 18.9	12	2	3	14 – 15	8
5.3 – 6.2	3	31.0 – 33.9	9	13.8 – 15.0	3	19.0 – 20.9	9	1	2	12 – 13	6
6.3 – 7.0	2	34.0 – 38.9	6	15.1 – 16.3	2	21.0 – 22.9	6	0	1	9 – 11	4
7.1 & over	1	39 & over	3	16.4 & over	1	23 & over	3			under 9	2

STAR TABLE

Total Points	Stars
46 & over	Champion Class
37 – 45	5
30 – 36	4
22 – 29	3
17 – 21	2
Under 17	1

2 For each test look up the points table to see how many points you have scored. For example, if you took 33.9 seconds on Test 2 (Turning) then this falls between 31 and 34 seconds and you would earn 9 points.

3 Write down your points in the table against each test.

4 Add up your points to get a Total.

5 Look up the Star Table to see how many stars you have gained (for example, if you scored 29 points you would have achieved a 3 ★★★ grade).

6 Record your Star Grade on page 65.

7 Set yourself a target to achieve the next time you are tested.

HOW WELL DID YOU DO?

1. **WRITE DOWN YOUR TEST RESULTS IN THIS TABLE.**
   RECORD THE TIMED TESTS TO 1/10th OF A SECOND.

UNDER 10'S

BE SURE TO CHECK THE CORRECT TABLE FOR YOUR AGE

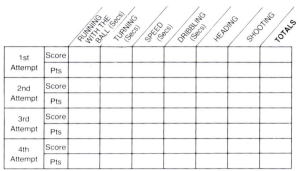

		RUNNING WITH THE BALL (Secs)	TURNING (Secs)	SPEED (Secs)	DRIBBLING (Secs)	HEADING	SHOOTING	TOTALS
1st Attempt	Score							
	Pts							
2nd Attempt	Score							
	Pts							
3rd Attempt	Score							
	Pts							
4th Attempt	Score							
	Pts							

Running with the ball		Turning		Speed		Dribbling		Heading		Shooting	
Time (secs)	Points	Time (secs)	Points	Time (secs)	Points	Time (secs)	Points	Goals	Points	Score	Points
under 4.6	5	under 27	15	under 12.9	5	under 16	15	3	10	16 & above	10
4.6 – 4.9	4	27.0 – 28.9	12	12.9 – 13.5	4	16.0 – 17.9	12	2	6	15	8
5.0 – 5.8	3	29.0 – 31.9	9	13.6 – 14.6	3	18.0 – 19.9	9	1	4	12 – 14	6
5.9 – 6.5	2	32.0 – 36.9	6	14.7 – 15.9	2	20.0 – 21.9	6	0	2	9 – 11	4
6.6 & over	1	37 & over	3	16.0 & over	1	22 & over	3			under 9	2

STAR TABLE

Total Points	Stars
52 & over	Champion Class
38 – 51	5
31 – 37	4
23 – 30	3
18 – 22	2
Under 18	1

2. For each test look up the points table to see how many points you have scored. For example, if you took 31.9 seconds on Test 2 (Turning) then this falls between 29 and 32 seconds and you would earn 9 points.
3. Write down your points in the table against each test.
4. Add up your points to get a Total.
5. Look up the Star Table to see how many stars you have gained (for example, if you scored 32 points you would have achieved a 3 ★★★ grade).
6. Record your Star Grade on page 65.
7. Set yourself a target to achieve the next time you are tested.

To master these techniques and score highly on the tests

★ **Running with the ball**
Play the ball well in front of you and chase after it.

★ **Turning**
Bend those knees.

Remember these key factors

★ **Speed**
Keep your head steady.

BE SURE TO CHECK THE CORRECT TABLE FOR YOUR AGE

HOW WELL DID YOU DO?

1 **WRITE DOWN YOUR TEST RESULTS IN THIS TABLE. RECORD THE TIMED TESTS TO 1/10th OF A SECOND.**

		RUNNING WITH THE BALL (Secs)	TURNING (Secs)	SPEED (Secs)	DRIBBLING (Secs)	HEADING	SHOOTING	TOTALS
1st Attempt	Score							
	Pts							
2nd Attempt	Score							
	Pts							
3rd Attempt	Score							
	Pts							
4th Attempt	Score							
	Pts							

Running with the ball		Turning		Speed		Dribbling		Heading		Shooting	
Time (secs)	Points	Time (secs)	Points	Time (secs)	Points	Time (secs)	Points	Goals	Points	Score	Points
under 4.4	5	under 26	15	under 12.5	5	under 15	15	3	10	16 & above	10
4.4 – 4.7	4	26.0 – 27.9	12	12.5 – 12.9	4	15.0 – 16.9	12	2	6	15 –	8
4.8 – 5.5	3	28.0 – 29.9	9	13.0 – 14.2	3	17.0 – 18.9	9	1	4	12 – 14	6
5.6 – 6.0	2	30.0 – 34.9	6	14.3 – 15.5	2	19.0 – 20.9	6	0	2	9 – 11	4
6.1 & over	1	35 & over	3	15.6 & over	1	21 & over	3			under 9	2

STAR TABLE

Total Points	Stars
52 & over	Champion Class
38 – 51	5
31 – 37	4
23 – 30	3
18 – 22	2
Under 18	1

2 For each test look up the points table to see how many points you have scored. For example, if you took 29.9 seconds on Test 2 (Turning) then this falls between 28 and 30 seconds and you would earn 9 points.
3 Write down your points in the table against each test.
4 Add up your points to get a Total.
5 Look up the Star Table to see how many stars you have gained (for example, if you scored 32 points you would have achieved a 3 ★★★ grade).
6 Record your Star Grade on page 65.
7 Set yourself a target to achieve the next time you are tested.

HOW WELL DID YOU DO?

1. **WRITE DOWN YOUR TEST RESULTS IN THIS TABLE. RECORD THE TIMED TESTS TO 1/10th OF A SECOND.**

BE SURE TO CHECK THE CORRECT TABLE FOR YOUR AGE

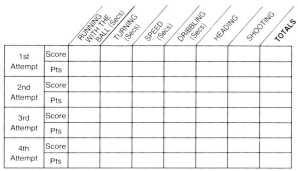

		Running with the ball		Turning		Speed		Dribbling		Heading		Shooting	
		Time (secs)	Points	Time (secs)	Points	Time (secs)	Points	Time (secs)	Points	Goals	Points	Score	Points
		under 4.3	5	under 24	15	under 11.0	5	under 14	15	3	10	17 & above	10
		4.3 – 4.5	4	24.0 – 25.9	12	11.0 – 12.5	4	14.0 – 15.9	12	2	6	16	8
		4.6 – 5.3	3	26.0 – 28.9	9	12.6 – 13.8	3	16.0 – 17.9	9	1	4	13 – 15	6
		5.4 – 5.7	2	29.0 – 32.9	6	13.9 – 15.1	2	18.0 – 19.9	6	0	2	10 – 12	4
		5.8 & over	1	33 & over	3	15.2 & over	1	20 & over	3			under 10	2

STAR TABLE

Total Points	Stars
52 & over	Champion Class
38 – 51	5
31 – 37	4
23 – 30	3
18 – 22	2
Under 18	1

2. For each test look up the points table to see how many points you have scored. For example, if you took 28.9 seconds on Test 2 (Turning) then this falls between 26 and 29 seconds and you would earn 9 points.
3. Write down your points in the table against each test.
4. Add up your points to get a Total.
5. Look up the Star Table to see how many stars you have gained (for example, if you scored 30 points you would have achieved a 3 ★★★ grade).
6. Record your Star Grade on page 65.
7. Set yourself a target to achieve the next time you are tested.

UNDER 13'S

BE SURE TO CHECK THE CORRECT TABLE FOR YOUR AGE

HOW WELL DID YOU DO?

1 **WRITE DOWN YOUR TEST RESULTS IN THIS TABLE. RECORD THE TIMED TESTS TO 1/10th OF A SECOND.**

		RUNNING WITH THE BALL (Secs)	TURNING (Secs)	SPEED (Secs)	DRIBBLING (Secs)	HEADING	SHOOTING	TOTALS
1st Attempt	Score							
	Pts							
2nd Attempt	Score							
	Pts							
3rd Attempt	Score							
	Pts							
4th Attempt	Score							
	Pts							

Running with the ball		Turning		Speed		Dribbling		Heading		Shooting	
Time (secs)	Points	Time (secs)	Points	Time (secs)	Points	Time (secs)	Points	Goals	Points	Score	Points
under 4.2	5	under 19	15	under 9.6	5	under 11	15	3	10	17 & above	10
4.2 – 4.4	4	19.0 – 23.9	12	9.6 – 12.1	4	11.0 – 12.9	12	2	6	16 –	8
4.5 – 5.2	3	24.0 – 27.9	9	12.2 – 13.4	3	13.0 – 16.9	9	1	4	13 – 15	6
5.3 – 5.5	2	28.0 – 29.9	6	13.5 – 14.7	2	17.0 – 18.9	6	0	2	10 – 12	4
5.6 & over	1	30 & over	3	14.8 & over	1	19 & over	3			under 10	2

STAR TABLE

Total Points	Stars
52 & over	Champion Class
38 – 51	5
31 – 37	4
23 – 30	3
18 – 22	2
Under 18	1

2 For each test look up the points table to see how many points you have scored. For example, if you took 27.9 seconds on Test 2 (Turning) then this falls between 24 and 28 seconds and you would earn 9 points.
3 Write down your points in the table against each test.
4 Add up your points to get a Total.
5 Look up the Star Table to see how many stars you have gained (for example, if you scored 30 points you would have achieved a 3 ★★★ grade).
6 Record your Star Grade on page 65.
7 Set yourself a target to achieve the next time you are tested.

HOW WELL DID YOU DO?

1. **WRITE DOWN YOUR TEST RESULTS IN THIS TABLE. RECORD THE TIMED TESTS TO 1/10th OF A SECOND.**

UNDER 14'S

BE SURE TO CHECK THE CORRECT TABLE FOR YOUR AGE

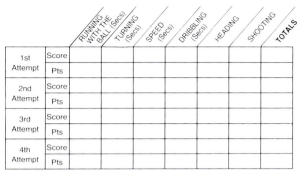

		RUNNING WITH THE BALL (Secs)	TURNING (Secs)	SPEED (Secs)	DRIBBLING (Secs)	HEADING	SHOOTING	TOTALS
1st Attempt	Score							
	Pts							
2nd Attempt	Score							
	Pts							
3rd Attempt	Score							
	Pts							
4th Attempt	Score							
	Pts							

Running with the ball		Turning		Speed		Dribbling		Heading		Shooting	
Time (secs)	Points	Time (secs)	Points	Time (secs)	Points	Time (secs)	Points	Goals	Points	Score	Points
under 4.1	5	under 18	15	under 8.6	5	under 10	15	3	10	17 & above	10
4.1 – 4.3	4	18.0 – 21.9	12	8.6 – 11.1	4	10.0 – 11.9	12	2	6	16 –	8
4.4 – 5.1	3	22.0 – 24.9	9	11.2 – 12.4	3	12.0 – 15.9	9	1	4	13 – 15	6
5.2 – 5.4	2	25.0 – 27.9	6	12.5 – 13.7	2	16.0 – 17.9	6	0	2	11 – 12	4
5.5 & over	1	28 & over	3	13.8 & over	1	18 & over	3			under 11	2

STAR TABLE

Total Points	Stars
52 & over	Champion Class
38 – 51	5
31 – 37	4
23 – 30	3
18 – 22	2
Under 18	1

2. For each test look up the points table to see how many points you have scored. For example, if you took 24.9 seconds on Test 2 (Turning) then this falls between 22 and 25 seconds and you would earn 9 points.
3. Write down your points in the table against each test.
4. Add up your points to get a Total.
5. Look up the Star Table to see how many stars you have gained (for example, if you scored 30 points you would have achieved a 3 ★★★ grade).
6. Record your Star Grade on page 65.
7. Set yourself a target to achieve the next time you are tested.

57

Remember these key factors

★ **Dribbling**
Pretend to go outside the markers but accelerate past them on the inside.

To master these techniques and score highly on the tests

★ **Shooting**   Keep the ball low. Aim for the far half of the goal.

★ **Heading**
Attack the ball – don't let it attack you.

BE SURE TO CHECK THE CORRECT TABLE FOR YOUR AGE

HOW WELL DID YOU DO?

1 **WRITE DOWN YOUR TEST RESULTS IN THIS TABLE. RECORD THE TIMED TESTS TO 1/10th OF A SECOND.**

		RUNNING WITH THE BALL (Secs)	TURNING (Secs)	SPEED (Secs)	DRIBBLING (Secs)	HEADING	SHOOTING	TOTALS
1st Attempt	Score							
	Pts							
2nd Attempt	Score							
	Pts							
3rd Attempt	Score							
	Pts							
4th Attempt	Score							
	Pts							

Running with the ball		Turning		Speed		Dribbling		Heading		Shooting	
Time (secs)	Points	Time (secs)	Points	Time (secs)	Points	Time (secs)	Points	Goals	Points	Score	Points
under 4.0	5	under 17	15	under 7.6	5	under 9	15	3	10	17 & above	10
4.0 – 4.2	4	17.0 – 19.9	12	7.6 – 10.1	4	9.0 – 10.9	12	2	6	16	8
4.3 – 5.0	3	20.0 – 22.9	9	10.2 – 11.4	3	11.0 – 14.9	9	1	4	14 – 15	6
5.1 – 5.3	2	23.0 – 25.9	6	11.5 – 12.7	2	15.0 – 16.9	6	0	2	11 – 13	4
5.4 & over	1	26 & over	3	12.8 & over	1	17 & over	3			under 11	2

STAR TABLE

Total Points	Stars
52 & over	Champion Class
38 – 51	5
31 – 37	4
23 – 30	3
18 – 22	2
Under 18	1

2 For each test look up the points table to see how many points you have scored. For example, if you took 22.9 seconds on Test 2 (Turning) then this falls between 20 and 23 seconds and you would earn 9 points.

3 Write down your points in the table against each test.

4 Add up your points to get a Total.

5 Look up the Star Table to see how many stars you have gained (for example, if you scored 30 points you would have achieved a 3 ★★★ grade).

6 Record your Star Grade on page 65.

7 Set yourself a target to achieve the next time you are tested.

HOW WELL DID YOU DO?

1. **WRITE DOWN YOUR TEST RESULTS IN THIS TABLE. RECORD THE TIMED TESTS TO 1/10th OF A SECOND.**

UNDER 16'S

BE SURE TO CHECK THE CORRECT TABLE FOR YOUR AGE

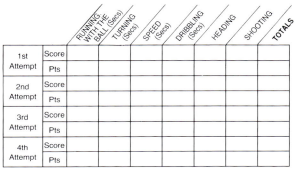

		RUNNING WITH THE BALL (Secs)	TURNING (Secs)	SPEED (Secs)	DRIBBLING (Secs)	HEADING	SHOOTING	TOTALS
1st Attempt	Score							
	Pts							
2nd Attempt	Score							
	Pts							
3rd Attempt	Score							
	Pts							
4th Attempt	Score							
	Pts							

Running with the ball		Turning		Speed		Dribbling		Heading		Shooting	
Time (secs)	Points	Time (secs)	Points	Time (secs)	Points	Time (secs)	Points	Goals	Points	Score	Points
under 3.9	5	under 16	15	under 6.6	5	under 8	15	3	10	17 & above	10
3.9 – 4.1	4	16.0 – 17.9	12	6.6 – 9.1	4	8.0 – 9.9	12	2	6	16	8
4.2 – 4.9	3	18.0 – 20.9	9	9.2 – 10.4	3	10.0 – 13.9	9	1	4	14 – 15	6
5.0 – 5.2	2	21.0 – 23.9	6	10.5 – 11.7	2	14.0 – 15.9	6	0	2	12 – 13	4
5.3 & over	1	24 & over	3	11.8 & over	1	16 & over	3			under 12	2

STAR TABLE

Total Points	Stars
52 & over	Champion Class
38 – 51	5
31 – 37	4
23 – 30	3
18 – 22	2
Under 18	1

2. For each test look up the points table to see how many points you have scored. For example, if you took 20.9 seconds on Test 2 (Turning) then this falls between 18 and 21 seconds and you would earn 9 points.
3. Write down your points in the table against each test.
4. Add up your points to get a Total.
5. Look up the Star Table to see now many stars you have gained (for example, if you scored 30 points you would have achieved a 3 ★★★ grade).
6. Record your Star Grade on page 65.
7. Set yourself a target to achieve the next time you are tested.

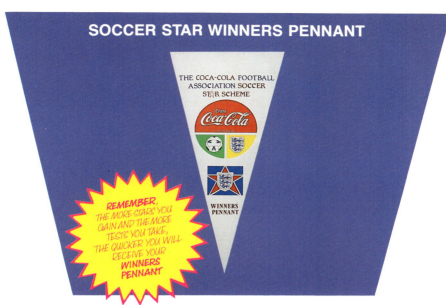

How to obtain your FREE Soccer Star Winners Pennant:

1 Collect the Red stars sent to you.

2 Stick these stars in the spaces provided on the next page.

3 When you have collected 20 stars and completed this page cut along the dotted line and send it with stamps to the value of 25p to:

The Soccer Star Office,
22/24a The Broadway,
Darkes Lane,
Potters Bar,
Herts EN6 2HH.

4 Do not rip this page out, merely cut where indicated.

5 Complete the following information:

NAME: _____

ADDRESS _____

_____

_____

Coca-Cola is a registered trade mark of The Coca-Cola Company

Your Soccer Star Winners Pennant will be sent to you by return of post.

STICK YOUR STARS HERE

REMEMBER, THE MORE STARS YOU GAIN AND THE MORE TESTS YOU TAKE, THE QUICKER YOU WILL RECEIVE YOUR WINNERS PENNANT.

1	2	3	4
5	6	7	8
9	10	11	12
13	14	15	16
17	18	19	20

Coca-Cola is a registered trade mark of The Coca-Cola Company